Contents

USING CHILDREN'S LITERATURE

A Whole-Language Approach
To Teaching Thinking Skills

Written by Vowery Dodd
Illustrated by Karen Neulinger

Educational Impressions

ISBN 0-910857-80-6

© 1991 Educational Impressions, Inc., Hawthorne, NJ

EDUCATIONAL IMPRESSIONS, INC.

Hawthorne, NJ 07507

FOREWORD

Using Children's Literature: A Whole-Language Approach to Teaching Thinking Skills uses ten popular children's books, including two Caldecott Medal winners, to develop important higher-level critical and creative thinking skills. Each unit contains a teacher help page with introductory questions and suggestions, a series of questions and activities based upon Bloom's *Taxonomy,** a fluency/flexibility activity, several extended-thinking shape cards, and a writing and/or sketching activity.

The units may be used in any order. You may want to use the *Mousekin's Golden House* unit just before or just after Halloween, but it may be used at any time. Also, these units are very flexible; use all or some of the activities depending on time limitations and the abilities of the youngsters in your class.

I really enjoyed writing this book. It has brought back my childhood days when I would sit on my mother's lap and listen to her read a story to me. I hope you and your class enjoy this book as much as I have.

Vowery Dodd

* Benjamin Bloom, *Taxonomy of Educational Objectives,* (New York: David McKay Company, Inc., 1956).

INTRODUCTION

Using Children's Literature: A Whole-Language Approach to Teaching Thinking Skills uses children's literature to teach children to read and think critically and creatively. An important part of each unit is the series of questions and activities based upon Bloom's *Taxonomy of Educational Objectives.** Bloom divided cognitive development into six main levels: knowledge, comprehension, application, analysis, synthesis, and evaluation. Most of the questions presented to students fall into the first two categories, knowledge and comprehension. The highest levels are seldom used; they are more difficult to write and, because they have no definite answer, are more difficult to evaluate. The following is a brief description of the cognitive levels according to Bloom's taxonomy.

Knowledge: This level involves the **simple recall** of facts stated directly.

Comprehension: The student must **understand** what has been read at this level. It will not be stated directly.

Application: The student uses knowledge that has been learned and **applies** it to a new situation. He/She must understand that knowledge in order to use it.

Analysis: The student **breaks down** learned knowledge into small parts and analyzes it. He/She will pick out unique characteristics and compare them with other ideas.

Synthesis: The student can now **create** something new and original from the acquired knowledge. This level involves a great deal of creativity.

Evaluation: The student makes a **judgment** and must be able to back up that judgment.

* Benjamin Bloom, *Taxonomy of Educational Objectives,* (New York: David McKay Company, Inc., 1956).

The shape activities are another integral part of each unit. They are designed to promote higher-level creative-thinking skills. Creative / productive thinking may be divided into five levels: fluency, flexibility, originality, elaboration, and evaluation. The activities in this book focus upon fluency, flexibility, and elaboration; these skills will be further explained.

Fluency involves listing as many different ideas as possible. As the child becomes proficient in this skill, a time limit may be applied. This forces the child to think more quickly while remaining creative. Sometimes children lose their ideas because of their inability to spell words correctly; therefore, younger children with limited spelling skills should be allowed to sketch their ideas rather than write them.

In fluency activities, brainstorming guidelines should be followed:

1. Criticism is ruled out.
2. Free-wheeling (using someone else's idea to come up with your own) is welcomed.
3. A quantity of ideas is encouraged.
4. Combination and improvement are sought.

The next level of creative / productive thinking is **flexibility.** This level deals with thinking in different categories. For example, suppose an activity involves listing things that are red. If the children list apples, beets, and radishes, they are thinking in only one category—food. When they begin to give answers like cars, birds, clothes, and houses, they are thinking in different categories; this type of thinking shows more flexibility. A scoring sheet is included on page 101 of this book. You may duplicate this sheet in order to keep track of the children's improvements in fluency and flexibility.

Elaboration is the addition of details to an idea. These details help create a better understanding of that idea. Elaboration may be done as a writing activity or as an art activity, in which case the youngsters add details to an illustration. Mind-mapping is a useful tool at this level.

Mind-mapping is a productive way to encourage children to participate in creative writing. It involves the taking of one idea and branching out with details about that idea. On the next page is an example of mind-mapping.

NOTE: The questions and activities in this book are easily adapted to meet the specific needs of your students. Except for the introductory discussion questions, most of the questions and activities may be done either at home or in the classroom. How independently the students work will depend upon your time limitations as well as the age and ability levels of the children.

Mind-Mapping

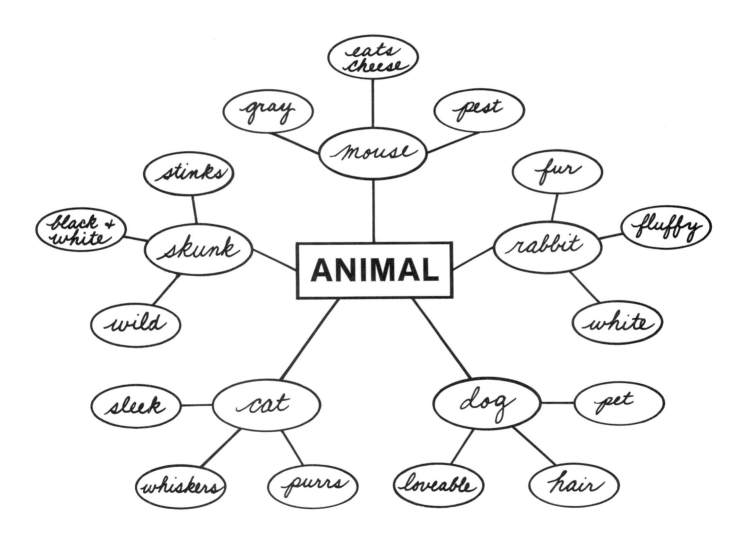

There's a Nightmare in My Closet

by Mercer Mayer

Begin this lesson by discussing the word *nightmare.* Ask the following questions:

1. What is a nightmare?

2. Is it real?

3. When do we usually have nightmares?

4. Where do nightmares come from?

After discussing these questions, read the story and discuss the questions based upon Bloom's Taxonomy. When you are finished, have the class do the fluency activity, Ways to Get Rid of a Nightmare. Duplicate and distribute the fluency/flexibility score sheet found on page 101. Have the children record their fluency scores. Help them if necessary. You will want to keep track of their improvement in this area. When this activity is completed, give everyone a Nightmare Hunter Badge. (See page 10.) Then continue with the rest of the activities.

The following books may be used to supplement this unit:

You're the Scaredy-Cat, by Mercer Mayer

Monster and the Baby, by Virginia Mueller

America's Very Own Monsters, by Daniel Cohen

My Mama Says There Aren't Any, by Judith Viorst

The Alligator Under the Bed, by Joan Lowery Nixon

Questions & Activities Based Upon Bloom's Taxonomy

There's a Nightmare in My Closet

Knowledge:
1. Who was in the boy's closet?
2. What did the boy do to the nightmare that caused it to cry?
3. When did the nightmare start to creep toward the boy?

Comprehension:
1. Explain what a nightmare is.
2. Describe some of the toys found in the boy's room.
3. Why did the boy let the nightmare in his bed?

Application:
1. Have you ever had a nightmare like the one in the story? Tell about it.
2. If you were a nightmare, where would you hide?
3. What would you have done to the nightmare?

Analysis:
1. Could there really be a nightmare like the one in the story? Why or why not?
2. Do you think the boy was really afraid of the nightmare? Why or why not?
3. Put yourself in the nightmare's place. How would you have felt when the boy pointed a gun at you? Why?

Synthesis:
1. Create and illustrate a new nightmare.
2. Plan another way for the boy to get rid of the nightmare.
3. Write a short paragraph (younger children can draw a picture) explaining what the nightmare does during the day.

Evaluation:
1. Was the boy's way of dealing with the nightmare good? Why or why not?
2. Can you think of a better way to end the story?
3. Do you like the illustrations in this story? Point out the illustrations you like or dislike; explain how you might change them.

2

Ways to Get
Rid of a Nightmare

List as many ways
as you can to get
rid of a nightmare.

3

**List as
many monsters
as you can.**

Sketch one.

List your
monsters here.

Sketch your
monster in this box.

_____

_____

_____

_____

_____

_____

_____

_____

_____

_____

_____

_____

_____

4

Make a list of
words used to
describe monsters.

Write your list here.

_____   _____

_____   _____

_____   _____

_____   _____

_____   _____

_____   _____

_____   _____

_____   _____

_____   _____

_____   _____

_____   _____

_____   _____

_____   _____

Write a paragraph about meeting a monster.

THE DAY I MET A MONSTER

_____

_____

_____

_____

_____

_____

_____

_____

_____

_____

_____

_____

Create a monster out of clay.

Write a description of your monster.

_____

_____

_____

_____

_____

_____

_____

_____

_____

_____

_____

_____

7

Write some
questions you
might like to
ask a monster.

I would like to ask . . .

1. _____

2. _____

3. _____

4. _____

5. _____

6. _____

Sketch
a nightmare.

9

Alexander and the Terrible, Horrible, No Good, Very Bad Day

by Judith Viorst

Alexander and the Terrible, Horrible, No Good, Very Bad Day is a wonderful book for helping children explore their feelings. Begin the lesson by discussing the different kinds of feelings people have. As the children mention the feelings, list them on the board. Then ask the children to describe various events that might lead to each of those feelings.

When the discussion has ended and the children seem to understand the feelings and emotions we all share, read the book to the class. Then have the children answer the questions on the following page. When all eighteen questions and activities have been completed, give the children copies of the three fluency activities: Things That Make Me Happy, Things That Make Me Sad, and Things That Make Me Angry. You may want to do these over a period of a few days. When the children have finished, have them count and record their fluency scores on the fluency/flexibility score chart. Help them if necessary.

At the end of this unit are Sketching Sheets and Writing/Sketching Sheets. Older children should be encouraged to both sketch and write about their feelings. Younger children may simply sketch in faces that represent their feelings each day.

Examples:

These activities will provide children with an opportunity to express their feelings and will make them aware that others, too, share these same feelings. They will also help children learn to deal with their many different emotions.

Questions & Activities Based Upon Bloom's Taxonomy

Alexander and the Terrible, Horrible, No Good, Very Bad Day

Knowledge:
1. What did Alexander have in his mouth when he went to sleep?
2. What did Alexander hope would happen to Paul?
3. What did Albert have in his lunch for dessert?

Comprehension:
1. Why was Alexander upset at breakfast?
2. Why did Mrs. Dickens like Paul's picture of a sailboat better than Alexander's picture of an invisible castle?
3. Explain why Alexander was so mad at Paul.

Application:
1. Have you ever had a day like Alexander's? Tell about it.
2. Alexander had problems at the dentist. Have you ever had a similar problem? Describe your experience.
3. How do you think you would have acted if you had had a day like Alexander's? Explain your feelings.

Analysis:
1. Compare Alexander's terrible day with a terrible day you have had. How was his day like or unlike your day?
2. Draw a picture that illustrates Alexander's horrible day.
3. How might you change the story to improve it? Explain.

Synthesis:
1. Create a new day for Alexander that won't be so terrible.
2. Plan a way for Alexander to get rid of his bad feelings as each horrible thing happens to him.
3. Make up some more terrible things that might happen to Alexander.

Evaluation:
1. Do you like the story about Alexander? Why or why not?
2. Why did Alexander want to go to Australia each time something terrible happened to him? Give reasons to support your answer.
3. Pretend to be Alexander's mother. What might she have done to make Alexander's day better?

12

Things That
Make Me Happy

List as many
things as you can
think of that make
you happy.

_____

_____

_____

_____

_____

_____

_____

_____

_____

_____

_____

_____

_____

_____

_____

13

Things That
Make Me Sad

List as many
things as you can
think of that make
you sad.

_____

_____

_____

_____

_____

_____

_____

_____

_____

_____

_____

_____

_____

_____

_____

_____

_____

14

Things That
Make Me Angry

List as many
things as you can
think of that make
you angry.

_____

_____

_____

_____

_____

_____

_____

_____

_____

_____

_____

_____

_____

_____

_____

_____

15

**Try to think
of the many
different feelings
that people have.
List those feelings.**

**In the space below list as many feelings
as you can think of.**

_____   _____

_____   _____

_____   _____

_____   _____

_____   _____

_____   _____

_____   _____

_____   _____

_____   _____

_____   _____

16

**Make a list of
words used to
describe a
happy feeling.**

Words used to describe a happy feeling are:

_____   _____
_____   _____
_____   _____
_____   _____
_____   _____
_____   _____
_____   _____
_____   _____
_____   _____
_____   _____

17

**Sketch a picture
of something
that makes
you happy.**

Sketch your picture in this box.

18

Pretend that your best friend is angry. How can you help your friend deal with that feeling?

I can help my friend by . . .

1. _____

_____

2. _____

_____

3. _____

_____

4. _____

_____

5. _____

_____

6. _____

_____

19

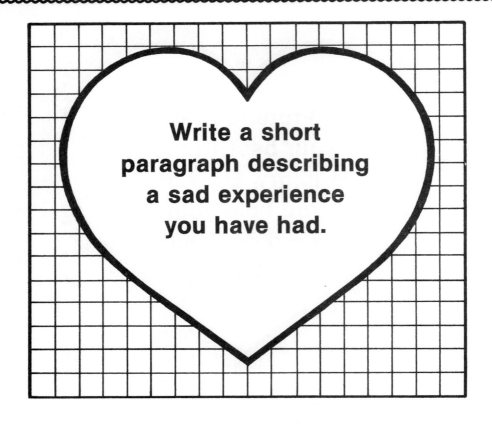

Write a short paragraph describing a sad experience you have had.

_____

_____

_____

_____

_____

_____

_____

_____

_____

_____

_____

_____

_____

Sketching Sheets

Keep track of your feelings for several days. Each day draw a face in the circle that shows how you feel.

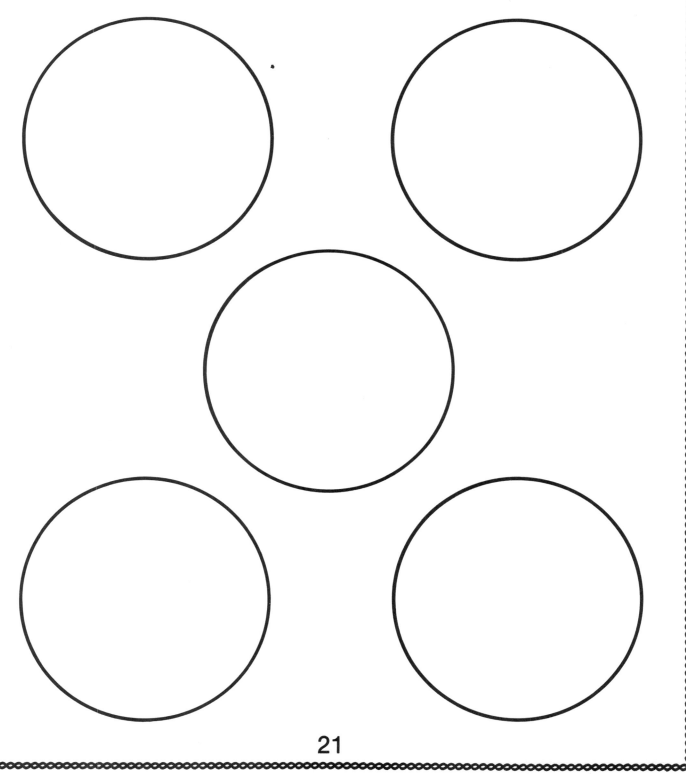

21

Writing/Sketching Sheets

Keep track of your feelings for several days. Each day draw a face in the circle that shows how you feel. In the space to the right of the circle, explain how you feel and why you feel that way.

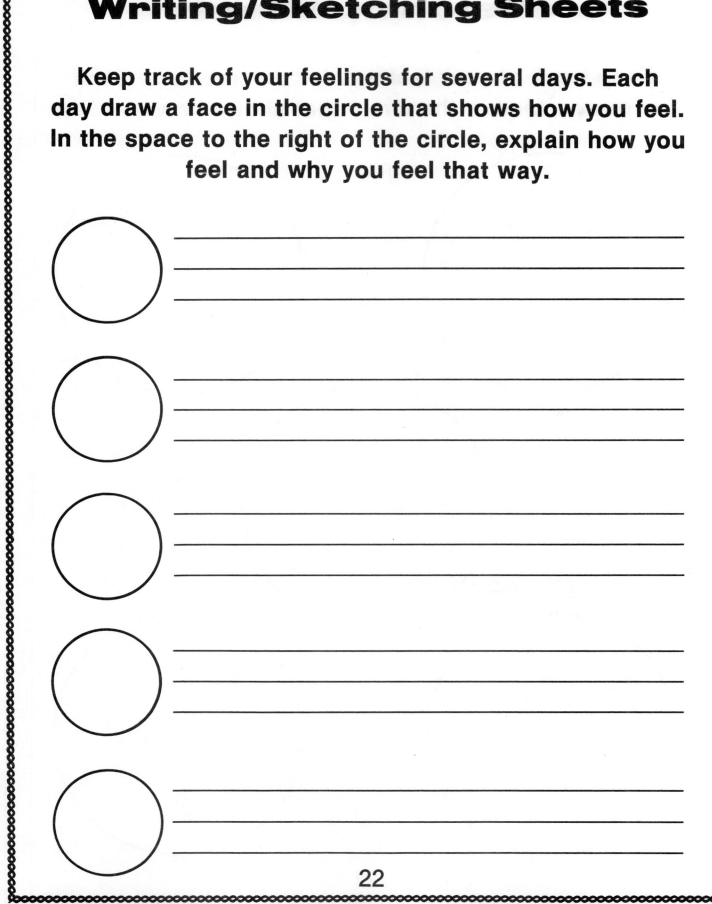

22

Just Me and My Dad

by Mercer Mayer

Begin this unit by discussing family trips. Ask questions such as

1. Does your family take trips together? If so, describe one of those trips.

2. What kind of trip would you like to take with your family?

After the introductory discussion, read the story to the class and discuss the questions based upon Bloom's Taxonomy. When all the questions have been answered and discussed, have the youngsters do the fluency activity, A Trip to the Country. Duplicate and distribute the fluency/flexibility score sheet. Have the children record their fluency scores. Help them if necessary. Then go on to the shape activities.

At the end of the unit there is a writing and sketching activity. Younger children with limited writing ability may omit the writing portion and just sketch a picture of a trip to the ocean if you prefer.

Questions & Activities Based Upon Bloom's Taxonomy

Just Me and My Dad

Knowledge:
1. Where were the father and son going?
2. Why couldn't they camp at the first campsite?
3. What did the father do before he and his son went to sleep?

Comprehension:
1. What happened to the canoe?
2. Why was the son afraid to go to sleep?
3. Do you think the son enjoyed eating the eggs? Why?

Application:
1. Have you ever been camping? If so, describe your trip.
2. Describe how the campsite might have looked.
3. List some things you might need to take with you on a camping trip.

Analysis:
1. If you were on a camping trip, which animal would you not want to see? Why?
2. What kinds of animals might have been hiding in the bushes?
3. Compare animals living in a forest with animals living in a desert. How are they alike and how are they different?

Synthesis:
1. Imagine that you are on a camping trip and that you are lost. What will you do?
2. Create a new adventure that the dad and his son might experience.
3. Pretend to go camping on the moon. Describe your trip.

Evaluation:
1. Does a hug ever make you feel better? Why?
2. Would you like to spend the night out in the forest? Why or why not?
3. What is your favorite thing to do with your mother or father? Why?

24

A Trip to the Country

List all the things you might see on a trip to the country.

_____   _____
_____   _____
_____   _____
_____   _____
_____   _____
_____   _____
_____   _____
_____   _____
_____   _____
_____   _____
_____   _____
_____   _____
_____   _____
_____   _____
_____   _____
_____

25

List as many uses for trees as you can. Categorize your list.

idea   category

26

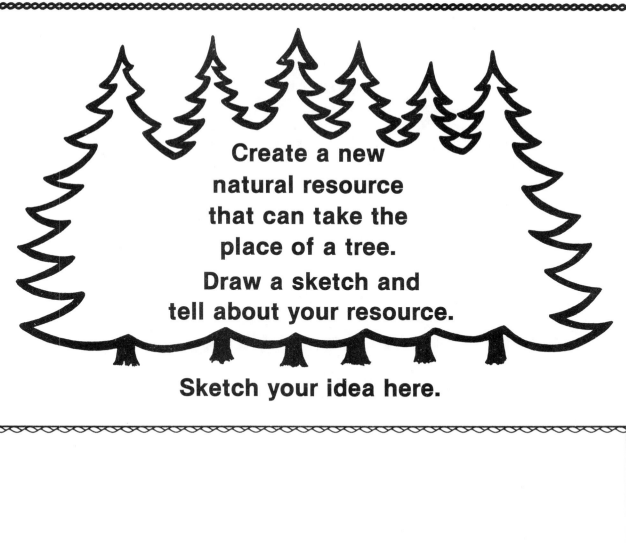

Create a new natural resource that can take the place of a tree.

Draw a sketch and tell about your resource.

Sketch your idea here.

27

Suppose all the water were to disappear from the forest. List some problems that might result. How might you help solve the problems?

Some of the problems might be . . .

1. _____
2. _____
3. _____
4. _____
5. _____

I might help solve the problems by . . .

_____
_____
_____
_____
_____

28

**Write a short
paragraph describing
sounds you might
hear in the woods.**

_____

_____

_____

_____

_____

_____

_____

_____

_____

_____

_____

_____

_____

_____

Design a new tent that would be easy to set up.

Sketch your idea in the box.

Sketch
a trip
to the ocean.

Write
about a trip to the ocean.

_____

_____

_____

_____

_____

_____

_____

_____

_____

_____

_____

_____

_____

_____

_____

_____

_____

_____

32

Mousekin's Golden House

by Edna Miller

Begin this lesson by discussing pumpkins. Ask the following questions:

    1. Which holidays are associated with pumpkins?

    2. What do many people do with pumpkins on Halloween?

    3. Did you ever carve a face into a pumpkin? If so, describe it.

    4. What do many people do with pumpkins on Thanksgiving?

    5. What season do you think of when you see a pumpkin?

After discussing these questions, read the story and present the questions based upon Bloom's Taxonomy. When all the questions and activities have been completed, have the class do the fluency activity, Pumpkins Galore. When they have finished compiling their lists, have them categorize their ideas on the big T activity sheet that follows.

Example of categorizing:

Things To Do With A Pumpkin

IDEA	CATEGORY
make pie	food
make a jack-o'-lantern	decoration
roast pumpkin seeds	food

When they are done, ask them to count their ideas and the different categories. Have them record the numbers on the fluency/flexibility score chart. Then have them go on to the shape activities.

33

Questions & Activities Based Upon Bloom's Taxonomy

Mousekin's Golden House

Knowledge:

1. What strange thing did Mousekin see?

2. What kind of a mouse is Mousekin?

3. Where did Mousekin jump when the owl swooped toward him?

Comprehension:

1. How did Mousekin get into his new home?

2. Describe in your own words Mousekin's new home.

3. Why did the cat run away?

Application:

1. How is Mousekin's house different from your house?

2. Show how Mousekin could have improved his house.

3. Draw a map of the forest and locate Mousekin's house.

Analysis:

1. Compare Mousekin's house to the chipmunk's. How are they alike and how are they different?

2. Write three questions you would like to ask Mousekin about why he chose the pumpkin for his winter home.

3. Arrange an experiment using a pumpkin. See how long it takes for the pumpkin to shrink. Find out why this happens.

Synthesis:

1. Create a new house for Mousekin.

2. Suppose Mousekin had chosen the hollow log for his home. How might he have made it comfortable?

3. Pretend Mousekin wants to rent part of his house. Write an advertisement for Mousekin to rent his house.

Evaluation:

1. Choose a character in the story to be Mousekin's friend. Tell why you chose that character.

2. Recommend this book to a friend. Give three reasons why someone would want to read this book.

3. Select a new title for the story. Give reasons for your choice.

34

Pumpkins Galore

List all the things you could do with a pumpkin. Try to think of some unusual things you might do with it as well as the ordinary things.

_____

_____

_____

_____

_____

_____

_____

_____

_____

_____

_____

_____

Pumpkins Galore

Now put your ideas into categories.

IDEA	CATEGORY

Sketch Mousekin in his pumpkin house.

Draw your picture here.

37

Create a design for a jack-o'-lantern. Add some interesting details.

Draw your jack-o'-lantern in the box.

38

List other animals that might use a pumpkin for a home.

These animals might use a pumpkin for a home:

_____

_____

_____

_____

_____

_____

_____

_____

_____

_____

39

Compare the
mouse's home
with your home.

**The mouse's home and my home are
alike in these ways:**

_____

_____

_____

_____

_____

_____

**The mouse's home and my home are
different in these ways:**

_____

_____

_____

_____

_____

_____

40

Tell what it would be like if you lived in a pumpkin.

_____
_____
_____
_____
_____
_____
_____
_____

_____
_____
_____
_____
_____

41

Suppose
you had to stay
in your house all
winter.

Write about what you would do to stay entertained.

_____

_____

_____

_____

_____

_____

_____

_____

_____

_____

_____

_____

_____

_____

_____

**On another sheet of paper
draw a picture to illustrate your story.**

A Giraffe and a Half

by Shel Silverstein

Begin this unit by discussing giraffes. Ask questions such as

1. How would you describe a giraffe?

2. Where do giraffes live?

3. Did you ever see a giraffe? Where?

4. What do giraffes eat?

After the introductory discussion, read the story to the class. Involve the children in the reading by letting them repeat the pattern. Use motions to help the youngsters remember each situation. The following are suggested motions:

With a rat in his hat—*point to your head*
Looking cute in a suit—*put your hands on your waist and wiggle your hips*
With a rose on his nose—*point to your nose*
And a bee on his knee—*point to your knee*
Playing toot on a flute—*pretend to play a flute*
With a chair in his hair—*pretend to comb your hair with your hands*
And a snake eating cake—*open and close your hand (4 fingers to thumb)*
And a skunk in a trunk—*hold your nose and say this in a nasal tone*
And a dragon in a wagon—*say this in a low, growling voice*
And a spike in his bike—*hold your fingers apart about 3 inches*
And a whale on his tale—*puff out your checks to represent a whale*
In a hole with a mole—*put your hand above your eyes and look down*

After the story has been read, discuss the questions based upon Bloom's Taxonomy. When all the questions and activities have been completed, have the youngsters do the fluency activity, Giraffe in a House. (It might be a good idea to elicit from the youngsters the inadvisability of keeping wild animals as pets before you do this activity.) Have the children record their fluency scores. Then go on to the shape activities.

Another interesting book you might want to read to the class is *Laugh with a Giraffe,* by Betty Jane Reed.

Questions & Activities Based Upon Bloom's Taxonomy

A Giraffe and a Half

Knowledge:
1. What lived in the giraffe's hat?
2. How did the giraffe look in his suit?
3. What did the dragon ride in?

Comprehension:
1. What happened to the giraffe when it stepped into the glue?
2. What would really happen to a bike if it ran over a spike?
3. Describe a whale.

Application:
1. How would you dress the giraffe if it belonged to you?
2. How would you act if a bee stung you?
3. If you stepped into glue, how would you get out?

Analysis:
1. How would having a giraffe be like having a pet dog or cat?
2. Compare the way a giraffe would feel living in Africa with the way it would feel living in a zoo or with you.
3. Why, do you think, did the author use a giraffe as the main character in this story? Explain your answer.

Synthesis:
1. Create a new ending for the book.
2. Create a pattern book using a different animal and different situations.
3. Pretend you have a giraffe that follows you everywhere. What could you do to keep the giraffe from following you around?

Evaluation:
1. Is it right to take a wild animal from its home and to put it into a zoo? Why or why not?
2. How do you feel about this story? Give reasons for your answer.
3. How would you feel if you were taken away from your home and family like the giraffe was? Give reasons for your answer.

44

Giraffe in a House

Pretend that you have a pet giraffe. It is beginning to rain and you want to get your giraffe into the house. How many different ways can you think of to get the giraffe into the house? Stretch your imagination and try to think of some unusual ideas.

Cut a new door.

45

For example:

plane – train
car – bar

List word pairs
that rhyme.

_____
_____
_____
_____
_____
_____
_____
_____
_____
_____
_____
_____
_____

46

For example:

A plane on a train.
A bar on a car.

_____
_____
_____
_____
_____
_____
_____
_____
_____
_____
_____
_____
_____

Use your rhyming words to create pattern sentences.

On another sheet of paper illustrate your sentences.

47

List animals
that are found
in the zoo.

48

Choose one zoo animal. Gather facts about that animal.

Share what you learn with the class.

49

Think about the animal you chose. Design a place for that animal to live.

On another sheet of paper draw a picture of your animal's new home.

Make the place like its real home.

50

Write
about another zoo animal you might like for a pet.

Write a story about your new pet.

_____

_____

_____

_____

_____

_____

_____

_____

_____

_____

_____

_____

_____

_____

_____

**On another sheet of paper
draw a picture to illustrate your story.**

51

Official Member of the Giraffe and a Half Club

Official Member of the Giraffe and a Half Club

Official Member of the Giraffe and a Half Club

Official Member of the Giraffe and a Half Club

52

The Sweet Touch

by Lorna Balian

Begin this unit by asking the following question: What if you had all the sweet treats you ever wanted? Elicit from the youngsters whether or not they would tire of eating them.

After discussing this question, read the story *A Sweet Touch,* by Lorna Balian. Then present the questions and activities based upon Bloom's Taxonomy. When they have been completed, have the class do the fluency activity, Sweet Things. When the children have finished compiling their lists, have them categorize their ideas on the big T activity sheet.

Example of categorizing:

Things That Are Sweet

IDEA	CATEGORY
candy	snack
ice cream	dessert
Jane	human

When the youngsters are done, ask them to count their ideas and the different categories. Ask them to record the numbers on the fluency/flexibility score chart. Have them compare these scores with previous scores to see if their fluency and flexibility skills have improved. Then proceed with the other activities.

53

Questions & Activities Based Upon Bloom's Taxonomy

The Sweet Touch

Knowledge:
1. What did Peggy get out of the gum machine?
2. What was the creature's name?
3. Where did the creature appear?

Comprehension:
1. Describe the creature that appeared after Peggy rubbed the ring.
2. Why did Peggy hide under the covers?
3. Explain why the genie could grant Peggy only one wish.

Application:
1. What would you do if a genie appeared to you?
2. Tell about another story that has a genie.
3. Plan an easier way for a genie to grant a wish.

Analysis:
1. Which do you think would have been better: wishing that you had a lot of money or wishing that everything you touched became something sweet? Explain.
2. Do you think Peggy's adventure really happened, or do you think she was just dreaming?
3. Identify good reasons why everything Peggy touched turned into sweets.

Synthesis:
1. Predict what might have happened if Peggy had wished for money instead of sweets.
2. Create a new way for Oliver to turn off the wish. Write it down and share it with the class.
3. What might have happened if Peggy had wished for a roomful of _____? Make up different things and explain what might have happened for each idea.

Evaluation:
1. Did Peggy make a wise choice with her wish? Explain.
2. Could this story really have happened? Why or why not?
3. What kind of person was the genie's mother? Give reasons for your answer.

54

Sweet Things

List all the things you can think of that are sweet. Try to think of some ideas that no one else will think of.

55

Sweet Things
Now put your ideas into categories.

IDEA	CATEGORY

List different
kinds of candy.

_____   _____
_____   _____
_____   _____
_____
_____
_____
_____
_____
_____
_____
_____
_____
_____

57

Sketch your favorite candy.

Draw your favorite candy in the candy dish.

58

Create a new kind of candy. Write a paragraph telling how you will make it and what it will taste like.

Ingredients:

_____   _____
_____   _____
_____   _____
_____   _____
_____

My candy . . . _____

_____
_____
_____
_____
_____
_____
_____
_____

List several reasons why people would want to buy your candy.

People would want to buy my candy because . . .

_____

_____

_____

_____

_____

_____

_____

_____

_____

_____

_____

_____

_____

60

Design an advertisement to sell your candy.

Sketch your idea here.

Plan
how you will make your new candy the best-selling candy in the country.

Describe what different things you will do to get people to buy more of your candy than any other kind.

_____

_____

_____

_____

_____

_____

_____

_____

_____

_____

_____

_____

_____

_____

**On another sheet of paper
draw a picture to illustrate your story.**

62

Owl Moon

by Jane Yolen

Discuss the CALDECOTT MEDAL with the children. Point out the seal on the book. Explain that a book receives the Caldecott Medal because of its illustrations. List and, if possible, bring in other books that have won the Caldecott Medal. Ask the following questions:

1. Have you read any books that have received the Caldecott Medal?

2. Have you read any books that you feel should have won the Caldecott Medal but did not?

3. How important are the illustrations to you?

Then ask these questions to introduce *Owl Moon:*

1. Have you ever seen an owl? Where?

2. What kind of sound does it make?

3. When do owls usually sleep? When are they active?

After discussing these questions, read the story. As you read point out the beautiful illustrations. Then present the questions based upon Bloom's Taxonomy. When these questions and activities have been completed, have the class do the fluency/flexibility activity, Things That Are Cold. When they have finished compiling their lists, ask them to categorize their ideas on the big T activity sheet that follows. Count and record the children's scores on the score sheet. Then proceed with the other activities.

Questions & Activities Based Upon Bloom's Taxonomy

Owl Moon

Knowledge: 1. What blew long and low?

2. What did the moon do to the father's face?

3. Where must you go to go owling?

Comprehension: 1. Describe an owling trip.

2. Explain what happened the first time the girl's father called the owl.

3. Describe the owl.

Application: 1. Have you ever hunted anything with your father or mother? Describe your experience.

2. What do you think the owl thought when the father shined the light on it?

3. Explain why the girl compared the clearing in the forest to milk.

Analysis: 1. Compare hunting owls in the forest with hunting cats in the alley. How are they alike and how are they different?

2. Describe how the girl felt when she saw her first owl.

3. List some disadvantages of owling.

Synthesis: 1. Design a trap that would catch an owl without hurting it.

2. Create another hunting adventure and write about it.

3. Suppose a snowstorm had come as the girl and her father were going home. What might have happened?

Evaluation: 1. Would you like to go owling? Why or why not?

2. Do you think the girl enjoyed her first owling trip? Explain your answer.

3. Would you want to catch an owl? Why or why not?

64

Things That Are Cold

List all the things you can think of that are cold.
Try to think of some unusual ideas.

_____
_____
_____
_____
_____
_____
_____
_____
_____
_____
_____
_____
_____
_____
_____
_____
_____
_____
_____
_____
_____
_____

65

Things That Are Cold

Now put your ideas into categories.

IDEA	CATEGORY

List words
that express
excitement.

These words express excitement:

_____ _____
_____ _____
_____ _____
_____ _____
_____ _____
_____ _____
_____ _____
_____ _____
_____ _____
_____ _____

67

Create a game called "Owling." Be sure to include rules for playing your game.

The object of my game is . . .

_____

_____

_____

_____

The rules of my game are . . .

_____

_____

_____

_____

_____

_____

Find out
more about owls.
Share the
information
with the class.

Some facts I learned about owls are:

1. _____

_____

2. _____

_____

3. _____

_____

4. _____

_____

5. _____

_____

6. _____

_____

70

Sketch
a picture about meeting an owl.

71

Write
a story about meeting an owl.

_____

_____

_____

_____

_____

_____

_____

_____

_____

_____

_____

_____

_____

_____

_____

_____

_____

_____

_____

_____

Hey, Al

by Arthur Yorinks

Hey, Al, written by Arthur Yorinks and illustrated by Richard Egielski, won the Caldecott Medal for 1987. (See page 63. If this unit is done before *Owl Moon,* discuss the Caldecott Medal before continuing.) It is an excellent book to initiate a discussion on occupations and about the important contributions made by all kinds of workers. It can also be used to stimulate children's thoughts about what a perfect paradise would be like. Before reading the book, discuss the following introductory questions:

1. What would you like to do when you grow up?

2. What causes people to be unhappy with their jobs?

3. What can people do to be happy about their work?

After discussing these questions, read the story. As you read point out the beautiful illustrations. Then present the questions based upon Bloom's Taxonomy. When these questions and activities have been completed, have the class do the fluency/flexibility activity, Many Different Jobs. When they have finished compiling their lists, ask them to categorize their ideas on the big T activity sheet that follows. Count and record the children's scores on the score sheet. Have the children see if they are improving their fluency and flexibility scores. Then proceed with the other activities.

At the end of the unit the children will be asked to write a paragraph and to draw a picture describing what they would like to be when they grow up. Younger children with limited writing ability may skip the writing portion and just sketch the picture.

Questions & Activities Based Upon Bloom's Taxonomy

Hey, Al

Knowledge:
1. What was Al's dog's name?
2. Who came to visit Al and his dog in the bathroom?
3. Where did Al's visitor take him and his dog?

Comprehension:
1. Describe Al's room.
2. Explain Al's job.
3. Why, do you think, was Al unhappy with his life?

Application:
1. If, like Al, you had the chance to visit a secret island, would you go?
2. Draw a map of Al's island.
3. Has anyone ever tried to get you to do something you knew was not right? Explain the situation.

Analysis:
1. Compare this story with the one about Pinocchio. How are they alike and how are they different?
2. How is this island like paradise? How is it different?
3. How did Eddie's feelings change after he began to change into a bird? Describe the change.

Synthesis:
1. Create your own special paradise. Illustrate it.
2. Develop a plan for Al to improve his life.
3. Predict how Al's life might have been different if he had become a bird.

Evaluation:
1. What kind of bird do you think Al would have been? Explain your reasons.
2. Was it a good idea for Al to go with the strange bird? Why or why not?
3. How might you change this story? Give reasons for your answer.

Many Different Jobs
List as many different kinds of jobs as you can.

_____

_____

_____

_____

_____

_____

_____

_____

_____

_____

_____

_____

_____

_____

_____

_____

_____

75

Many Different Jobs
Now put your ideas into categories.

IDEA	CATEGORY

Draw a cartoon that describes Al's adventure.

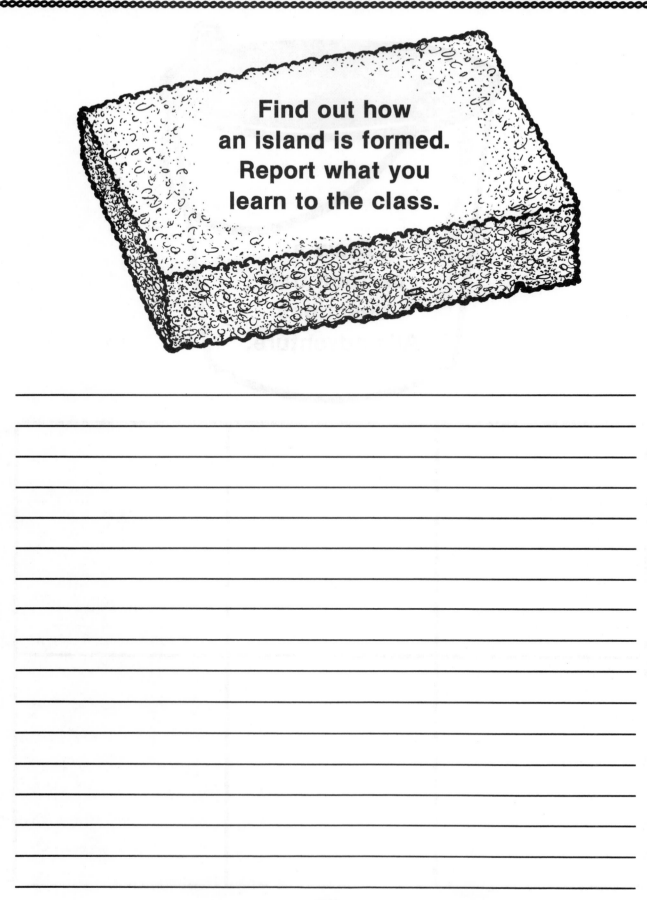

**Find out how
an island is formed.
Report what you
learn to the class.**

_____

_____

_____

_____

_____

_____

_____

_____

_____

_____

_____

_____

_____

_____

_____

Pretend to be a newspaper reporter. A man with wings has been seen flying across the ocean. Write an article.

79

Invent a new job for Al that he will like. Sketch a picture of Al doing his new job.

80

Sketch
a picture . . .

What will I be when I grow up?

Write
a paragraph . . .

What will I be when I grow up?

_____

_____

_____

_____

_____

_____

_____

_____

_____

_____

_____

_____

_____

Patrick's Dinosaurs

by Carol Carrick

Patrick's Dinosaurs, written by Carol Carrick and illustrated by Donald Carrick, is a very good book with which to introduce a science unit on dinosaurs. Begin by asking the following questions:

1. How did dinosaurs look? (Elicit from the youngsters that although some of the dinosaurs were the largest creatures ever to roam the earth, not all of the dinosaurs were big.)

2. Are any dinosaurs alive today?

3. Where did they all go?

4. Do you know what the word *extinct* means? (If none of the children know, explain the term to them.)

5. Have you ever seen dinosaurs in a museum? Describe what you saw.

After discussing these questions, read the story. Then present the questions based upon Bloom's Taxonomy. When these questions and activities have been completed, have the children do the fluency/flexibility activity, Things That Are Big. When they have finished compiling their lists, ask them to categorize their ideas on the big T activity sheet that follows. Count and record the children's scores on the score sheet. Then proceed with the other activities.

At the end of the unit is a writing/sketching activity. The youngsters will be asked to write about their favorite dinosaur, giving characteristics and details about it and its environment. They will then be asked to draw a picture. Younger children with limited writing skills can go right to the sketching part of the activity and omit the writing portion.

As an optional activity, you might want to assign one or both of the following projects:

1. Design a dinosaur out of clay.

2. Make a diorama of a dinosaur in its environment.

Questions & Activities Based Upon Bloom's Taxonomy

Patrick's Dinosaurs

Knowledge:
1. How many elephants weigh the same as a brontosaurus?
2. How much bigger were prehistoric crocodiles than today's crocodiles?
3. Name two of the prehistoric animals in this book.

Comprehension:
1. Describe a tyrannosaurus.
2. Why did Patrick see the tyrannosaurus in his window?
3. Describe the prehistoric animal's environment.

Application:
1. List several objects that might be the same size as a stegosaurus.
2. Describe how prehistoric birds might have looked.
3. Have you ever been to a zoo? Illustrate a picture of a zoo that you have visited or would like to visit.

Analysis:
1. Compare the brontosaurus with a lizard. How are they alike and how are they different?
2. Identify some possible reasons for the disappearance of the dinosaurs many years ago.
3. Why, do you think, were some of the prehistoric animals so much bigger than today's animals?

Synthesis:
1. Create a new prehistoric animal. Describe and sketch it.
2. What would the world be like today if the dinosaurs had not become extinct?
3. Pretend to be a reporter for a radio station. Write a report about a brontosaurus found living in the park.

Evaluation:
1. Which prehistoric animal is your favorite? Why?
2. Would you like to live in a world with dinosaurs and other prehistoric animals? Why or why not?
3. If you found a baby stegosaurus, would you keep it and raise it, or would you give it to a zoo? Explain.

Things That Are Big

List as many things as you can that are big.
Use your imagination. Think of unusual ideas.

85

Things That Are Big

Now put your ideas into categories.

IDEA	CATEGORY

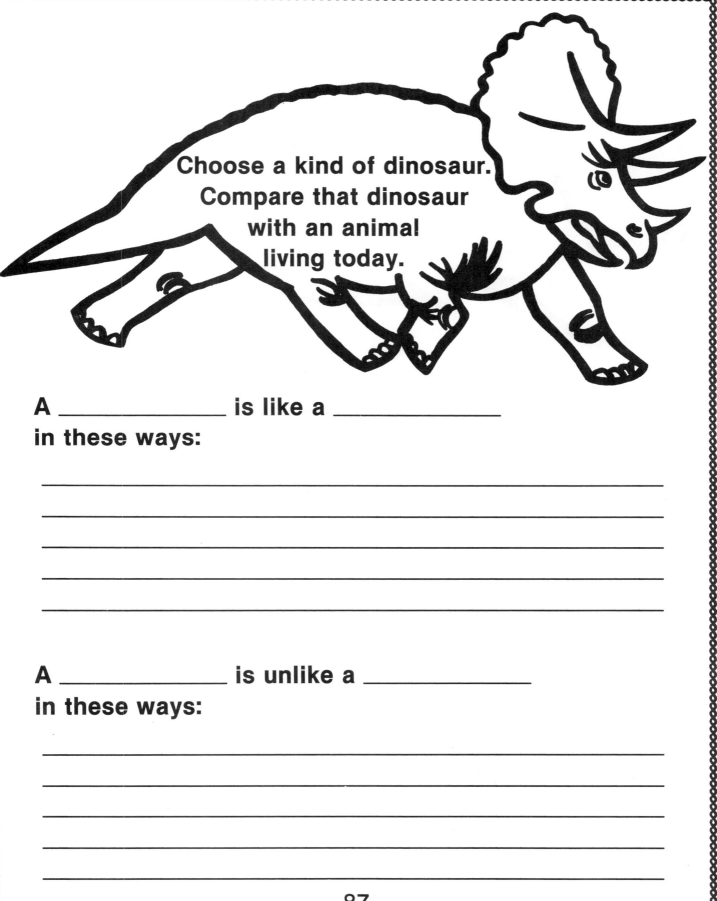

Choose a kind of dinosaur. Compare that dinosaur with an animal living today.

A _____ is like a _____
in these ways:

_____
_____
_____
_____
_____

A _____ is unlike a _____
in these ways:

_____
_____
_____
_____
_____

87

Create an unknown island
where dinosaurs still live.
Sketch that island.
Show the dinosaurs.

88

If you could have a pet dinosaur, which one would you choose?

_____

_____

_____

_____

_____

_____

_____

_____

_____

_____

_____

_____

Give your dinosaur a name. Describe how you would take care of it. Where would you keep it?

89

Write
about your favorite dinosaur.

_____

_____

_____

_____

_____

_____

_____

_____

_____

_____

_____

_____

_____

_____

_____

_____

**On another sheet of paper
draw a picture of your favorite dinosaur.**

90

The Gigantic Balloon

by Ruth Park

The Gigantic Balloon, written by Ruth Park, is a good book with which to introduce a unit on consumerism. Begin by asking the following questions:

1. What causes us to go into a store and buy something?

2. How many of you have seen commercials on television? Do the commercials make you want to buy the products they advertise? How?

3. Do commercials always tell the truth?

4. Did you ever buy something and then find out that the product was not what you had expected it to be?

After discussing these questions, read the story. Then present the questions based upon Bloom's Taxonomy. When these questions and activities have been completed, have the children do the fluency/flexibility activity, Things We Buy. When they have finished compiling their lists, ask them to categorize their ideas on the big T activity sheet that follows. Count and record the children's scores on the score sheet. Compare these scores with the earlier ones to see if their fluency and flexibility skills have improved. Then proceed with the other activities.

At the end of the unit is a writing activity. The youngsters will be asked to invent a product and to write a commercial for it. You may want to have them present their commercials as if they were recording them for radio or television. If so, you may prefer to have them work in small groups to prepare and present their skits.

Questions & Activities Based Upon Bloom's Taxonomy

The Gigantic Balloon

Knowledge:
1. Who was Peter Thin?
2. What did Peter want to become?
3. What was Peter's dog's name?

Comprehension:
1. What kind of stores did Mr. Hoy and Mr. Jones own?
2. Explain how Mr. Hoy tried to get people to buy from him.
3. Explain why the balloon would not float up at first.

Application:
1. If you had a store, how would you get people to buy your products?
2. List other things that can fly without a motor.
3. Have you ever had a pet that you felt very close to? Tell about your pet.

Analysis:
1. Compare Mr. Hoy and Mr. Jones. How are they alike and how are they different?
2. What kind of businessmen do you think Mr. Hoy and Mr. Jones are? Explain your answer.
3. Why, do you think, did Mr. Jones want Peter to pretend to be a Frenchman?

Synthesis:
1. Create an advertisement for Mr. Jones's store that would make people want to buy from him.
2. Describe Peter's life after he left in the balloon.
3. Change the story so that Mr. Hoy and Mr. Jones become partners. How will the story be different?

Evaluation:
1. Should Peter have taken the balloon? Why or why not?
2. What kind of men were Mr. Hoy and Mr. Jones? Give reasons for your answer.
3. Who do you think was the better salesman, Mr. Hoy or Mr. Jones? Why?

92

Things We Buy

Try to think of all the different kinds of things we buy.
List those things.

_____   _____
_____   _____
_____   _____
_____   _____
_____   _____
_____   _____
_____   _____
_____   _____
_____   _____
_____   _____
_____   _____
_____   _____
_____   _____
_____   _____

93

Things We Buy

Now put your ideas into categories.

IDEA	CATEGORY

94

List things
that can be found
in the air.
Categorize your list.

idea **category**

Compare air transportation with ground transportation.

Air transportation and ground transportation are alike in these ways:

_____

_____

_____

_____

_____

_____

Air transportation and ground transportation are different in these ways:

_____

_____

_____

_____

_____

_____

Design and sketch a new form of air transportation.

97

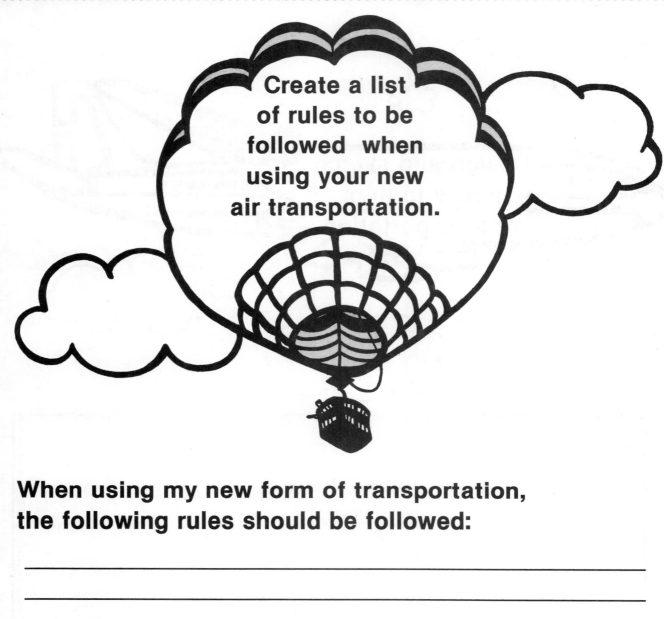

Create a list
of rules to be
followed when
using your new
air transportation.

When using my new form of transportation, the following rules should be followed:

_____

_____

_____

_____

_____

_____

_____

_____

_____

_____

98

Design an advertisement that will make everyone want to use your air transportation.

Invent
a new product. Write a radio or television commercial for your product.

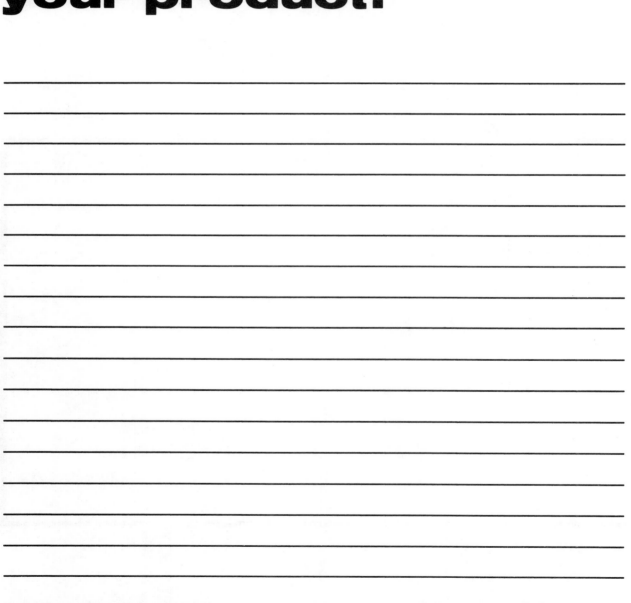

_____

_____

_____

_____

_____

_____

_____

_____

_____

_____

_____

_____

_____

_____

_____

_____

FLUENCY & FLEXIBILITY SCORE SHEET

Name _____ **Grade** _____

Activity	Fluency	Flexibility
Ways to Get Rid of a Nightmare	_____	_____
Things That Make Me Happy	_____	_____
Things That Make Me Sad	_____	_____
Things That Make Me Angry	_____	_____
A Trip to the Country	_____	_____
Pumpkins Galore	_____	_____
Giraffe in a House	_____	_____
Sweet Things	_____	_____
Things That Are Cold	_____	_____
Many Different Jobs	_____	_____
Things That Are Big	_____	_____
Things We Buy	_____	_____

Note: If these are done out of order, you might want to write in the date each is done.

BIBLIOGRAPHY

Balian, Lorna. *The Sweet Touch.* New York: Abingdon Press, 1988.

Carrick, Carol. *Patrick's Dinosaurs. New York: Clarion Books/Ticknor Fields, 1983.*

Mayer, Mercer. *Just Me and My Dad.* New York: Western Publishing Company, Inc., 1977.

—. *There's a Nightmare in My Closet.* New York: Dial Press, 1968.

Miller, Edna. *Mousekin's Golden House.* Englewood Cliffs, NJ: Prentice-Hall, Inc., 1964.

Park, Ruth. *The Gigantic Balloon.* New York: Parents' Magazine Press, 1977.

Silverstein, Shel. *A Giraffe and a Half.* New York: Harper & Row Publishers, 1064.

Viorst, Judith. *Alexander and the Terrible, Horrible, No Good, Very Bad Day.* New York: Atheneum, 1972.

Yolen, Jane. *Owl Moon.* New York: Philomel Books, 1987.

Yorinks, Arthur. *Hey, Al.* New York: Farrar, Straus and Giroux, 1987.

SUPPLEMENTAL READING

Cohen, Daniel. *America's Very Own Monsters.* New York: Dodd, 1982.

Mayer, Mercer. *You're the Scaredy-Cat.* New York: Parents' Magazine Press, 1974.

Mueller, Virginia. *Monster and the Baby.* Niles, IL: A. Whitman, 1985.

Nixon, Joan Lowery. *The Alligator Under the Bed.* New York: Putnam, 1974.

Reed, Betty Jane. *Laugh with a Giraffe.* Minneapolis: Denison, 1977.

Viorst, Judith. *My Mama Says There Aren't Any.* New York: Macmillan, 1973.